# The Workbook of Love for Couples in Relationship

*A Romance and Marriage Therapy Guide - Proven Strategies & Activities for Intimacy, Communication, Conflict Resolution, and Trust*

BY

Amanda Robinett

# The Workbook of Love for Couples in Relationship

BY

**Amanda Robinett**

# DISCLAIMER

This book is intended to give general information only. While every effort has been made to ensure the accuracy and completeness of the information provided, the Author makes no representations or warranties of any kind, express or implied, about the completeness, accuracy, reliability, suitability, or availability concerning the content contained within these pages.

Nothing in this book should be construed as a substitute for competent legal, financial, or other expert assistance. Readers are invited to seek the advice and counsel of specialists in the many subjects covered in this book to get precise answers to their questions and concerns.

If you use this book, you accept the conditions stated above. The Author and publisher take no responsibility for any problems that may arise from following the advice in this book.

# Table of Contents

# INTRODUCTION

Effective communication, intimacy, and trust are the essential threads that bind partners together in the complex dance of partnerships. However, a lot of couples deal with difficulties that sometimes seem impossible. Whether a couple is just starting in their relationship, navigating the turbulent waters of dispute, or looking to strengthen their existing link, this workbook is meant to be a source of hope and direction. Couples can improve the dynamics of their relationship by interacting with the exercises and ideas on these pages, transforming possible obstacles into chances for development and closeness.

This workbook's material demonstrates a thorough comprehension of typical relationship difficulties. Couples may feel like they are facing insurmountable barriers, such as miscommunication and emotional distancing. But this workbook does more than just point out these difficulties—it offers workable, doable answers to deal with them. The book's format combines academic information with practical exercises to guarantee that readers will not only understand their relationship dynamics better but will also actively work to improve them. Every chapter offers a thorough method for fostering and fortifying your relationship, building on the one before it.

There are detailed instructions on how to use the content in this workbook to get the most out of it. The reflections and exercises in this section are beneficial for both individuals and couples. It is recommended that partners approach this workbook with an open mind and a dedication to honesty and vulnerability. The process of reading and working through this material is an invitation to develop empathy, rekindle a passion that may have faded with time, and enhance your understanding of one another. It is not just a problem-solving exercise.

In the end, this workbook functions as a resource for partners looking to cultivate a happier, more satisfying union. You are taking the initiative to build a relationship that is based on love, understanding, and respect for one another by investing time and energy into the ideas and activities discussed here. As you set out on your adventure together, keep in mind that love is an ongoing process that thrives on shared experiences and a dedication to development. By working together, you may make your relationship a lively and long-lasting partnership that can handle life's challenges together.

# CHAPTER 1:

# THE FOUNDATION OF LOVE:

# UNDERSTANDING EACH OTHER'S

# NEEDS

In any relationship, the cornerstone of love lies in the ability to recognize, understand, and meet each other's emotional and practical needs. Each partner brings their own set of requirements into the relationship, shaped by their past experiences, personal values, and unique expectations. To build a stronger connection and ensure that both partners feel appreciated and understood, it is essential to identify and communicate these needs openly.

Couples who actively engage in this process create a foundation for a thriving relationship defined by mutual respect, understanding, and support. In this chapter, you will be guided through the crucial process of identifying and expressing your own needs as well as those of your partner, fostering a deeper and more meaningful connection.

## Understanding Your Own Needs and Those of Your Partner

Every successful relationship is built on the awareness and fulfillment of both emotional and practical needs. Emotional needs often include love, appreciation, affection, and emotional support. Practical needs, on the other hand, can involve shared responsibilities, financial security, or effective communication. To cultivate a healthy and balanced relationship, it is essential for each partner to take time to understand their own needs and those of their partner.

When you are aware of your needs, you can articulate them more clearly within the relationship. Self-awareness empowers you to communicate openly about what you need, leading to a greater sense of partnership. In turn, understanding your partner's needs allows you to create a

shared emotional and practical foundation that
your connection.

## Exercise: Identifying Emotional and Practical Needs

Think about what you need emotionally and practically in
your relationship. Each partner should take separate sheets
of paper and write down the five most important emotional
needs you have.

Once you have completed your lists, set aside time with your
partner to share and discuss each other's needs. This exercise
encourages vulnerability, fosters honest communication,
and lays the groundwork for deeper conversations.

## How Unfulfilled Needs Can Lead to Dissatisfaction and Conflict

When emotional or practical needs go unmet in a
relationship, it can lead to frustration, resentment, and even
conflict. If one partner feels their needs are not
acknowledged or valued, they may begin to feel neglected,
leading to emotional distance. Over time, these feelings can
erode trust and create an environment where conflict is
more likely to arise.

For example, imagine a scenario where one partner deeply values quality time together, but their partner's busy work schedule consistently limits their ability to connect. Over time, the partner who craves quality time may feel sidelined or unimportant. This emotional gap can create feelings of unworthiness or abandonment, which, if left unaddressed, can lead to a breakdown in communication and affection.

It is crucial to recognize the importance of addressing each other's needs to avoid this kind of disconnection. When both partners actively work to fulfill each other's emotional and practical needs, they create an environment where both individuals can thrive.

## Exercise: Reflecting on Unmet Needs

Reflect on a time when your needs were not met in your relationship. What were those needs, and how did it make you feel? How did it impact your connection with your partner? Take separate sheets of paper and write down your thoughts.

This exercise will help you better understand the emotional consequences of unmet needs and encourage open dialogue with your partner to prevent future misunderstandings.

# The Power of Empathy in Understanding Your Partner's Needs

Empathy is a powerful tool that bridges emotional gaps and fosters deeper understanding in any relationship. Empathy means making an effort to truly understand your partner's perspective, feelings, and needs. It requires active listening and a genuine desire to see the world through your partner's eyes.

When you approach your partner's needs with empathy, you validate their feelings and experiences. This creates a safe and supportive environment where both partners feel understood and appreciated. Empathy not only strengthens emotional bonds but also encourages vulnerability and trust, which are critical components of a successful relationship.

## Exercise: Practicing Empathy

Now that you've reflected on your own needs, take some time to practice empathy with your partner. Set aside a quiet moment to discuss how each of you feels when your needs are met versus when they are not. Use the following prompts to guide your conversation:

*"When my needs are met, I feel: _____"*

During this conversation, take turns speaking and listening without interrupting. Make sure each partner feels heard and understood before moving on to the next step. This exercise allows you to step into your partner's emotional landscape, promoting a deeper, more compassionate connection.

## Real-Life Example: A Journey Toward Mutual Understanding

Consider Sarah and John's story. Sarah placed great importance on spending quality time together to feel connected, but John's demanding career often got in the way. Over time, Sarah began to feel neglected, and this emotional distance led to resentment. She felt that her needs were being overlooked, while John, unaware of the depth of her feelings, assumed everything was fine.

Finally, Sarah voiced her concerns, and they had an open discussion about their needs. John realized how important quality time was to Sarah and made efforts to adjust his schedule. Sarah, in turn, recognized John's need for space to focus on his work. Together, they found a balance that honored both of their needs, strengthening their relationship.

This example highlights the importance of open communication and empathy in addressing unmet needs before they lead to conflict.

## Summary

Understanding and communicating both your own needs and those of your partner are essential for building a strong, healthy relationship. Emotional and practical needs form the foundation of connection, and when these needs are acknowledged and fulfilled, couples experience deeper intimacy and partnership.

Unmet needs, if left unaddressed, can lead to frustration, conflict, and emotional withdrawal. However, by practicing empathy and engaging in open communication, couples can navigate these challenges and cultivate a more harmonious relationship.

# CHAPTER 2:

# REKINDLING COMMUNICATION: THE ART OF TALKING AND LISTENING

The ability to communicate is essential to the success of every relationship because it acts as the key that enables partners to connect. Not only does communication include the words that are stated, but it also includes the feelings that are communicated and the comprehension that is shared. Building trust, settling disagreements, and cultivating intimacy all require effective communication as core components. On the other hand, ineffective communication can result in misunderstandings, feelings of bitterness, and, ultimately, the dissolution of the partnership. This chapter emphasizes the importance of rekindling communication as a fundamental component within the context of a healthy relationship. By exploring various aspects of communication, such as active listening, empathy, and the avoidance of typical barriers, partners can enhance their interactions and foster a deeper connection **(Lerner, H. 2004)**.

## Active vs. Passive Communication

To cultivate healthy conversations, it is vital to understand the difference between active and passive communication. Active communication involves openly engaging in dialogue, clearly expressing thoughts and emotions, and seeking feedback from the other partner. Success here requires both partners to be fully present and genuinely interested in what the other has to say. In contrast, passive communication involves hiding feelings, avoiding conflict, or downplaying personal needs. This type of interaction often leads to misunderstandings and unresolved issues. Passive communication can make partners feel ignored or unacknowledged, resulting in emotional distance over time. Recognizing the importance of active communication and transitioning toward it can significantly improve the quality of discussions and strengthen emotional connections between partners.

## Reflect on Your Own Communication Style

Use the space below to note which communication style you tend to use—active or passive. Think about recent interactions and write down how you usually respond in conversations.

## My Communication Style:

Partner 1

_____

Partner 2

_____

# Empathy and Nonverbal Communication

Empathy plays a crucial role in effective communication. It promotes understanding and compassion, enabling couples to connect on a deeper emotional level. When one partner shares their feelings or concerns, the other should strive to understand their emotional state and temporarily set aside their own opinions to achieve full comprehension. This approach fosters an environment where both partners feel supported and validated. Nonverbal communication—such as body language, facial expressions, and tone of voice—

often conveys more than words. Partners must be mindful of their nonverbal cues because these signals can significantly affect how messages are received. For example, maintaining eye contact and using open body language can signal attentiveness and respect, thereby strengthening the empathetic bond during conversations **(Chapman, G. 2015)**.

## Reflect on Your Nonverbal Cues

Take a moment to think about how you use nonverbal communication in your interactions. Write down examples of how you show empathy or attentiveness nonverbally.

## My Nonverbal Cues:

Partner 1

_____

Partner 2

_____

# Avoiding Communication Barriers

Communication barriers, such as criticism and assumptions, can hinder open dialogue and cause tension between partners. Assumptions occur when one partner makes judgments about the other's thoughts or feelings without confirming them, often leading to misunderstandings. For instance, assuming your partner is upset simply because they are quiet could lead to conflict if the assumption is inaccurate. Instead, couples should seek clarification by asking about each other's viewpoints and showing genuine curiosity about their partner's perspective. Criticism is another common barrier that can erode communication and trust. To avoid this, partners should express concerns using "I" statements to focus on their feelings rather than criticizing the other person. For example, instead of saying, "You always cancel our plans," a more positive approach would be, "I feel hurt when plans change unexpectedly." By consciously eliminating these barriers, partners can create a more open and supportive communication environment.

## Identify Your Communication Barriers

Write down any communication barriers you notice in your relationship. Think about times when assumptions or criticism may have affected your communication and note any changes you'd like to make.

## My Communication Barriers:

Partner 1

_____

Partner 2

_____

## Active Listening Exercise

Participating in active listening exercises can help develop communication skills. In this exercise, one partner speaks for a set amount of time—such as five minutes—about a topic or concern that is important to them, while the other partner listens without interruption. The listener's goal is to absorb what is being said, reflect back what they have heard, and ask clarifying questions if needed. After the speaking time is up, the listener should summarize the key points to ensure they have understood correctly. This exercise encourages the expression of thoughts and highlights the importance of being fully present during conversations. Through active listening, partners can foster deeper empathy and understanding, improving the quality of their communication.

## Reflection on Active Listening

After completing the active listening exercise, take a moment to reflect on the experience. Write down any insights or observations from the exercise, focusing on how it impacted your communication and understanding.

### My Reflection:

Partner 1

_____

Partner 2

_____

# Communication Style Quiz

Understanding each partner's communication style can greatly enhance interactions. Taking a Communication Style Quiz, which categorizes communication into assertive, passive, and aggressive styles, can help identify each person's approach. Each partner answers a series of questions designed to highlight tendencies in various situations. After completing the quiz, they should discuss the results together. This conversation will shed light on how each partner communicates and may identify areas for improvement. For instance, a passive communicator may struggle to voice their thoughts, while an assertive communicator confidently expresses their needs. Recognizing these styles helps increase understanding and cooperation, leading to more productive interactions.

## Instructions:

Each partner should take a separate sheet of paper and answer each question below with the letter that best describes their answer.

When expressing a concern, do you:

A) State your feelings clearly and openly
B) Try to keep the peace and avoid confrontation
C) Express your feelings strongly and sometimes with frustration

When you disagree with your partner, do you:

A) Calmly share your perspective and ask for theirs
B) Hold back your thoughts to avoid conflict
C) Raise your voice or get defensive if you feel strongly about it

When your partner has a different opinion, do you:

A) Listen and try to understand their perspective

B) Avoid saying much because you dislike arguments

C) Focus on convincing them of your view

When you feel hurt by something your partner said, do you:

A) Communicate your feelings respectfully

B) Avoid mentioning it to keep the peace

C) Express it in a way that might sound confrontational

## Scoring:

- Mostly A's: Assertive Style
- Mostly B's: Passive Style
- Mostly C's: Aggressive Style

## Interpreting Your Results

Once you've identified your communication style, use the space below to reflect on what this might mean for your relationship. Discuss any areas where you'd like to make changes.

## My Communication Style and Reflections:

Partner 1

_____

Partner 2

---

## Summary

Communication is a skill that must be continually honed and nurtured to foster a thriving relationship. By distinguishing between active and passive communication, couples can significantly enhance their interactions, ensuring both partners' voices are heard. Empathy and nonverbal communication further enrich these interactions, fostering a deeper emotional connection. Additionally, identifying and avoiding common communication barriers—such as criticism and assumptions—are essential for maintaining an open and supportive environment. The active listening exercise and communication style quiz presented in this chapter offer practical tools for partners to improve their communication skills. Each effort toward improving communication lays the foundation for a more fulfilling and lasting relationship overall.

# CHAPTER 3:

# EMOTIONAL INTIMACY: BUILDING CONNECTION THROUGH VULNERABILITY

In romantic partnerships, emotional intimacy forms the foundation for meaningful connections, allowing partners to genuinely comprehend and support each other. It extends beyond physical attraction or casual conversations, enabling individuals to share their innermost thoughts, emotions, and vulnerabilities. The development of trust, mutual respect, and an overall improvement in relationship quality are key outcomes of emotional intimacy. Without this essential component, couples risk drifting apart and struggling to connect on a deeper level. This chapter underscores the importance of emotional intimacy, exploring how vulnerability can fortify bonds, the role of emotional support and validation, and the practical steps that couples can take to create a safe space for open emotional expression.

## Strengthening Bonds Through Emotional Vulnerability

Emotional vulnerability involves the willingness to openly share one's true feelings, fears, and insecurities with a partner. While it can feel intimidating, embracing vulnerability is crucial for fostering emotional intimacy. When partners are transparent about their vulnerabilities, it encourages reciprocity, creating an environment where both feel safe and understood. This mutual openness deepens the connection, as partners witness each other's authentic selves. Vulnerability also plays a pivotal role in building trust, where one partner's courage to be open often inspires the other to do the same, reinforcing emotional closeness. Through emotional vulnerability, partners can better support each other through life's challenges and appreciate shared moments of joy. In essence, vulnerability weaves the threads that hold relationships together.

## The Power of Emotional Support and Validation

Emotional support is indispensable to emotional intimacy. It involves being there for one another during tough times, offering understanding and reassurance. Validation is a vital aspect of this process—acknowledging and respecting a partner's feelings without judgment or dismissal. When a partner feels validated, they are more likely to open up, confident that their emotions are recognized and valued. This creates a cycle of support where both partners feel encouraged to express their feelings and experiences. When couples lay this foundation of emotional support, they can navigate conflicts more effectively and deepen their understanding of one another's perspectives.

## Creating a Safe Space for Emotional Expression

For emotional intimacy to flourish, it's crucial to establish a safe environment for emotional expression. Couples can begin by setting ground rules for communication: actively listening without interruption, refraining from criticism, and respecting each other's emotions. Choosing the right time and setting for deeper conversations is equally important, ensuring both partners feel comfortable and ready to engage. Encouraging each other to express even the most uncomfortable emotions fosters a safe space for vulnerability. Patience and empathy are key, reinforcing the idea that it's okay to be vulnerable and that each partner's feelings are valid. By cultivating this safe space, couples enable emotional intimacy to grow, leading to a stronger, more resilient relationship.

## Emotional Check-In Exercises

The Emotional Check-In exercise provides a structured opportunity for partners to explore and express previously unvoiced emotions. Partners can set aside a weekly time to openly share their thoughts and feelings, with each taking turns speaking uninterrupted. The listener's role is to practice active listening, offering supportive feedback and validation. After both partners have shared, they can reflect on how these emotions impact their relationship and discuss ways to support each other through them. This exercise aims to deepen emotional intimacy while highlighting the importance of maintaining open emotional communication.

## Developing an Emotional Support Plan

Creating an Emotional Support Plan allows couples to proactively establish strategies for providing emotional support. Partners can begin by discussing their individual emotional triggers or challenges. From there, they can brainstorm ways to offer support during those times. For example, one partner may need a listening ear after a stressful workday, while another may seek comfort during moments of self-doubt. These strategies should be clearly documented and revisited regularly to ensure that both partners feel heard and supported. The Emotional Support Plan helps couples better understand each other's needs and reinforces the importance of being intentional with emotional support **(Lerner, H. 2004)**.

## Summary

Emotional intimacy is at the heart of a couple's connection and understanding. By embracing emotional vulnerability, partners can strengthen their bond and foster an environment where both feel valued and supported. The importance of emotional support and validation cannot be overstated, as these elements create a secure space for self-expression and encourage ongoing dialogue. Through exercises like the Emotional Check-In and the Emotional Support Plan, couples can intentionally cultivate emotional intimacy, enhancing the resilience of their relationship and their overall satisfaction. By embarking on this journey of emotional exploration, partners will discover that deeper intimacy and connection are both empowering and transformative.

# CHAPTER 4:

# CONFLICT RESOLUTION: TURNING

# ARGUMENTS INTO OPPORTUNITIES

Conflict is an inevitable part of any romantic relationship, and learning to resolve it constructively can deepen the bond between partners. Far from being a sign of dysfunction, healthy conflict—when handled with care, respect, and open communication—can serve as an opportunity for growth and understanding. In this chapter, we explore the significance of respectful communication, the role of emotional validation, and practical techniques for transforming disagreements into avenues for closeness and trust. By implementing conflict resolution strategies, couples can foster an environment where both individuals feel valued and understood.

## Respect and Consent in Conflict Resolution

Respect and consent are not only essential in physical intimacy but also crucial in resolving conflicts. Consent, in this context, means agreeing to engage in difficult conversations at times when both partners feel ready and are willing participants. In the same way that boundaries are important for physical intimacy, it is crucial for couples to set boundaries in conflict discussions, which could include time limits for difficult conversations or agreeing to pause and resume discussions when emotions have settled. Respectful communication ensures that both partners feel comfortable to express themselves without fear of judgment or escalation. By respecting each other's boundaries and comfort levels during conflict, couples lay the groundwork for constructive conversations that focus on understanding rather than winning. Conflict becomes an opportunity to grow when consent and respect create a safe environment for each partner to openly share their perspective.

## The Role of Emotional Connection in Conflict Resolution

Conflict resolution is deeply tied to the emotional connection between partners. Emotional distance can heighten misunderstandings and foster resentment, making it harder to approach conflicts with empathy and patience. Couples who work to understand each other's emotional needs and actively listen during disagreements are better equipped to navigate conflicts without alienating one another. Addressing emotional disconnection is crucial, as unresolved issues may lead to recurring arguments that detract from intimacy. When couples recognize that emotional support is an integral part of conflict resolution, they can approach disagreements with a spirit of cooperation, reducing feelings of isolation and building a more resilient partnership **(Sbarra, 2008)**.

## Techniques for Turning Arguments into Opportunities

Transforming conflicts into opportunities requires intentional effort, but couples can implement specific techniques to foster a constructive approach to disagreements. One effective technique is active listening, which involves focusing fully on the partner's perspective before responding. Paraphrasing the partner's words and asking clarifying questions can help avoid misunderstandings. Another technique is using "I" statements instead of "you" statements—for example, saying, "I feel hurt when I am interrupted" rather than, "You never listen to me." This approach helps partners express their feelings without triggering defensiveness. Couples can also agree on a "cool-down" strategy, where they take a short break if an argument becomes too heated, allowing both parties to regain composure and reapproach the conversation calmly. By viewing arguments as learning moments, partners can uncover and address underlying issues that, if left unexamined, might lead to greater disconnect.

## Touch Preferences as Conflict Soothers

While the Touch Preferences exercise primarily enhances physical intimacy, it can also play a supportive role in conflict resolution. By understanding each other's touch preferences, couples can leverage physical closeness as a means of comfort during or after conflicts. Physical touch— such as a hand on the shoulder or a supportive hug—can signal reassurance and help de-escalate tension. However, it is essential to remember that touch as a comfort should be consensual and only used when both partners are receptive. Through the integration of touch as a nonverbal method of showing support, partners can strengthen their emotional connection, making conflicts feel less adversarial and more collaborative.

## Conflict Resolution Calendar

Similar to the Intimacy Building Calendar, the Conflict Resolution Calendar is a tool for couples who wish to proactively address issues before they escalate. This calendar involves setting aside regular check-ins to discuss minor grievances, unmet needs, or other points of tension. By consistently dedicating time to open conversations, couples can address issues before they build up into larger conflicts. Examples of activities in the calendar may include weekly "state of the relationship" talks, gratitude exercises, or mutual goal-setting discussions that help both partners stay aligned. The calendar should be flexible to accommodate each partner's comfort level and availability, ensuring that both parties feel respected and valued.

Through constructive conflict resolution, couples can transform arguments into opportunities for growth, trust-building, and intimacy. Respectful communication, emotional validation, and proactive tools such as the Conflict Resolution Calendar empower partners to view disagreements not as threats to the relationship but as moments of shared growth. By committing to these practices, couples can cultivate a more harmonious relationship that can weather the inevitable challenges of life together.

## Summary

Conflict is a natural part of any relationship, but when approached with respect and understanding, it becomes an opportunity for growth and deeper intimacy. Healthy conflict resolution starts with setting clear boundaries and gaining mutual consent to engage in challenging conversations. This ensures that both partners feel safe and respected.

A strong emotional connection is vital for resolving conflicts constructively. Unresolved emotions can create recurring issues and widen the emotional gap between partners. By focusing on emotional validation and practicing empathy, couples can reduce misunderstandings and foster a spirit of cooperation.

# CHAPTER 5:

# TRUST: BUILDING AND REBUILDING

# AFTER BREACHES

Trust is the bedrock of any healthy and robust relationship. It forms the foundation on which all other components—communication, closeness, and emotional connection—are built. When trust is strong between two people, it fosters feelings of safety, reliability, and emotional security. Conversely, when trust is breached, it can create deep emotional wounds and sow seeds of doubt and uncertainty. In this chapter, we will explore why trust is vital to the longevity of relationships, delve into how couples can rebuild trust after experiencing betrayal or disappointment, and offer practical strategies for maintaining trust through transparency and honesty. Whether trust has been broken or remains intact, establishing and maintaining it requires ongoing effort from both partners.

## The Importance of Trust for Long-Term Relationships

Trust acts as the glue that holds a relationship together, creating an environment where both partners feel safe enough to be vulnerable with each other. It allows individuals to connect emotionally, share their deepest fears and desires, and depend on one another during difficult times. Without trust, the foundation of a relationship becomes shaky, leading to uncertainty, doubt, and anxiety. Trust allows both partners to relax into the relationship, knowing they can count on one another. This sense of security is crucial for the long-term durability of the relationship, laying the groundwork upon which love, communication, and intimacy can thrive. The ability to trust one another strengthens the emotional bond between partners and helps them weather the inevitable storms that occur in long-term commitments **(Fisher, 2004)**.

# Rebuilding Trust After Betrayal or Disappointment

Rebuilding trust after it has been damaged is undoubtedly difficult, but not impossible. When betrayal occurs—whether through infidelity, dishonesty, or broken promises—both partners are deeply affected. The betrayed partner often feels hurt, angry, and uncertain about whether they can trust again, while the partner who violated the trust may experience guilt and regret. The first step in the rebuilding process is acknowledging the breach and taking full responsibility for it. This involves offering a sincere apology, demonstrating genuine remorse, and showing a willingness to make amends.

Open communication is key at this stage, as both partners must discuss what happened and how it made each feel. Avoid rushing to fix things or brushing the issue under the rug (Perel, 2017).

The next phase of rebuilding trust is demonstrating consistent behavior. Trust cannot be restored by words alone; it must be proven through actions. The partner who broke the trust must consistently show reliability and dependability over time. This might include being more transparent, honoring commitments, and being mindful of the other person's emotional needs. Rebuilding trust is a gradual process that requires patience and dedication from both partners. Forgiveness is also an important part of this journey. While forgiveness does not mean forgetting the betrayal, it does involve letting go of resentment and focusing on building a better future together.

## Maintaining Trust Through Transparency and Honesty

Maintaining trust in a relationship requires continuous effort from both partners. One of the most effective ways to keep trust intact is through ongoing transparency and honesty. Transparency means being open about thoughts, feelings, and actions, even when it's uncomfortable to do so. It involves sharing key aspects of your life, such as your finances, future plans, or emotional state, without hiding or censoring information. When both partners practice transparency, it minimizes the chances of misunderstandings and prevents feelings of betrayal from creeping in.

Honesty is equally critical. Being truthful, especially in difficult conversations, builds trust over time because it shows respect for your partner and the relationship. This doesn't mean being brutally honest in a way that is hurtful, but rather being clear and sincere about your feelings, needs, and boundaries. Keeping your word and following through on commitments is another way to maintain trust. Consistently honoring promises creates a track record of reliability. Regular check-ins and discussions about how you can continue to trust and support each other are also essential for nurturing and growing trust.

## Trust-Scale Exercises

The Trust Scale Test offers a practical method for couples to evaluate and discuss trust within their relationship across key areas: finances, communication, emotional and physical intimacy, support during difficult times, and honesty/transparency. This exercise encourages open, meaningful conversations that help couples identify strengths and areas for improvement.

### Instructions for Completing the Trust Scale Test

Rating Trust in Key Areas: Each partner should independently rate their level of trust in each area below on a scale of 1 to 10, where:

1 = Very low trust

10 = Complete trust

**Categories to Rate:**

**Finances:** Trust in managing, sharing, and discussing financial matters.

**Communication:** Trust in each other's ability to communicate honestly and openly.

**Emotional Intimacy:** Trust in feeling emotionally supported and understood.

**Physical Intimacy:** Trust in feeling safe, respected, and valued in physical interactions.

**Support During Difficult Times:** Trust in each other's support during challenging situations.

**Honesty and Transparency:** Trust that each partner is truthful and transparent.

**Recording Scores:** Partners should write down their scores for each category but keep them private until both are ready to share.

**Discussing Results:** Set aside a specific time to exchange and discuss scores, focusing on areas with significant differences or lower scores. This conversation should be approached with empathy and a shared goal of understanding and strengthening the relationship.

## Interpreting the Results

**High Scores (8-10):** Indicate strong trust in this area. Acknowledge these strengths, as they are the foundation of your relationship.

**Mid Scores (5-7):** Suggest that trust is present but could benefit from improvement. Discuss specific ways to strengthen this area, such as setting goals or working on communication skills.

**Low Scores (1-4):** Signal that trust may be a significant concern. Approach these areas with sensitivity and consider discussing specific experiences or behaviors that may have affected trust. This may also be an opportunity to explore tools for rebuilding trust or consider counseling for additional support.

## Conclusions and Action Steps

The Trust Scale Test can help couples recognize their relationship's strengths and identify areas needing attention. By discussing each area and setting goals for improvement, couples can work together to rebuild trust and strengthen their partnership for lasting stability.

## The Rebuilding Trust Plan

For couples who have experienced a breakdown in trust, the Rebuilding Trust Plan provides a practical framework for healing. This exercise encourages both partners to sit down and create a strategy for rebuilding trust. The partner who broke the trust outlines specific steps they will take, such as being more transparent, keeping promises, or being more emotionally present. Both partners communicate what they need to feel safe and what actions they want to see to support the trust-rebuilding process. This plan gives the couple concrete steps to follow as they work through the healing process.

## Summary

Trust is the foundation of any healthy, long-lasting relationship. It allows couples to face challenges together, builds emotional security, enhances connection, and paves the way for deeper intimacy. However, trust is fragile, and once broken, it requires time, dedication, and persistent effort to be repaired. By acknowledging the breach, taking responsibility, and demonstrating consistent, trustworthy behavior, couples can heal and rebuild trust. Transparency and honesty are crucial for maintaining trust, and regular communication ensures both partners remain aligned. Trust, whether carefully nurtured or painstakingly rebuilt, requires ongoing care to grow and strengthen over time.

# CHAPTER 6:

# MANAGING EXPECTATIONS: ALIGNING

# YOUR VISIONS

Expectations significantly influence the dynamics of any relationship, impacting how partners connect, communicate, and resolve issues. However, unmet or uncommunicated expectations can lead to frustration, disappointment, and discontent. Often, couples are unaware of the unconscious expectations they bring into the relationship, which may not always be reasonable or grounded in reality. This chapter explores the importance of managing expectations effectively to maintain harmony and avoid unnecessary conflict. When couples understand the difference between reasonable and unrealistic expectations and learn how to align them with reality, they can build a relationship that meets both partners' aspirations and goals.

## Causes of Frustration: Unmet and Unrealistic Expectations

One of the primary sources of conflict in relationships stems from unmet expectations. People often enter romantic relationships with preconceived notions—sometimes consciously, sometimes unconsciously—about how their partner should behave, how the relationship should progress, and their role within it. These expectations are shaped by past experiences, family dynamics, societal norms, and personal goals. If these expectations are not openly communicated, they can become hidden "time bombs" waiting to explode.

Unrealistic expectations, such as believing your partner should never make mistakes or should intuitively know what you need without being told, are especially harmful. They set an unachievable standard, making it impossible for either partner to succeed. Over time, unmet expectations can lead to feelings of disappointment and frustration, as one or both partners feel their needs are not being met. Left unaddressed, this frustration can grow into resentment, emotional distance, and communication breakdowns.

## Differentiating Between Reasonable and Unreasonable Expectations

It's crucial to distinguish between reasonable expectations and those that are unrealistic. Reasonable expectations are based on mutual respect, clear communication, and a realistic understanding of each partner's capabilities. For instance, expecting emotional support during difficult times or equal contribution to household responsibilities are examples of fair and achievable expectations.

In contrast, unreasonable expectations often stem from idealized views of relationships or from standards that are unattainable, often shaped by media portrayals or societal pressures. Examples of these include expecting your partner to always agree with you, never have flaws, or be solely responsible for your happiness. These unrealistic demands put unnecessary strain on the relationship and make it difficult for either partner to feel successful in meeting the other's needs. Recognizing the distinction between reasonable and unreasonable expectations is essential for fostering a healthy, balanced relationship in which both partners feel valued and understood **(Sbarra, 2008)**.

# Aligning Expectations with Reality

Aligning expectations with reality begins with self-awareness and honest communication. Both partners should take time to reflect on what they want from the relationship and have open discussions about it. Recognizing that no relationship is perfect, and that both partners have strengths and weaknesses, is key to this process. It's important to accept that your partner cannot fulfill all of your needs, and that compromise is a natural part of any relationship.

One way to align expectations is through ongoing discussions about individual and shared goals. These conversations help couples check in with each other, adjust expectations as circumstances change, and ensure they are on the same page. By openly discussing expectations, couples can avoid disappointment and work together to create a realistic and achievable vision for their future. Aligning expectations doesn't mean sacrificing your needs, but rather finding a middle ground that respects both partners' needs and abilities.

# The Expectation Inventory Exercise

The Expectation Inventory is a helpful exercise that allows couples to identify and discuss previously unspoken expectations. In this exercise, each partner takes time to reflect and write down their expectations for the relationship on separate sheets of paper.These can include aspects such as emotional support, financial contributions, communication styles, physical intimacy, and future goals. After completing their lists, the couple comes together to share and discuss each item.

This exercise fosters open communication and allows each partner to express their needs and desires clearly. As they share their expectations, they can also assess which are reasonable and which may need adjustment. By the end of the exercise, couples gain a deeper understanding of each other's perspectives and are better equipped to align their expectations, creating a more harmonious relationship.

## Setting Goals Together

Goal setting is another key exercise that helps couples align their visions for the future. After completing the Expectation Inventory, partners can use this exercise to set shared goals that reflect both their individual aspirations and their collective vision for the relationship. These goals can be short-term, such as improving communication or spending more quality time together, or long-term, such as planning for financial security, starting a family, or collaborating on personal or professional endeavors.

Each partner should first identify their goals for the relationship, and then work together to create a list of shared goals. This process encourages collaboration and ensures that both partners feel invested in the relationship's future. Once goals are set, couples should develop actionable steps to achieve them. Regular check-ins will help track progress and allow for adjustments as needed.

## Summary

Managing expectations is essential for maintaining long-term harmony in any relationship. Unmet or unrealistic expectations often lead to frustration, dissatisfaction, and conflict, while clear and reasonable expectations create the foundation for a fulfilling partnership. By recognizing the difference between reasonable and unrealistic expectations and working together to align them with reality, couples can build a strong foundation of mutual respect and understanding.

# CHAPTER 7:

# FORGIVENESS: THE PATH TO HEALING

Forgiveness is a transformative process that plays a vital role in healing and moving forward in a relationship, particularly after disagreements, misunderstandings, or betrayals. It is essential to the healing process because it often requires a deep emotional reckoning, making it one of the most challenging components of maintaining a strong connection. Forgiveness is not about excusing or tolerating harmful behavior but rather a conscious decision to let go of the anger, hurt, and resentment that can weigh heavily on both parties. We will explore the true meaning of forgiveness, how to practice it toward oneself and one's partner, and the power it holds in releasing relationships from the past and fostering their growth.

## What Forgiveness Really Means (It's Not About Excusing Behavior)

At its core, forgiveness is about freeing yourself from the emotional burden of holding onto past hurts. Contrary to the misconception that forgiveness excuses someone's behavior, it's truly about releasing yourself from that burden. Forgiving someone is not about condoning their actions or forgetting what happened, but rather about letting go of the control that the pain and anger have on you and your relationship. By choosing forgiveness, you allow space for healing and enable the relationship to progress without being weighed down by unresolved issues.

Forgiveness is a process that requires time and effort, demanding genuine repentance, open communication, and a commitment to change. It's not a one-time event but an ongoing journey that involves self-reflection, empathy, and a willingness to rebuild trust. Both partners must acknowledge the pain caused and commit to working together to avoid repeating the same mistakes in the future.

## Techniques for Forgiving Both Yourself and Your Partner

Self-forgiveness is just as important as forgiving your partner. Often, individuals carry guilt or self-blame for their role in conflicts, leading to a cycle of shame and self-punishment. This can result in emotional withdrawal, resentment, and further breakdowns in communication. To truly heal, practicing self-compassion is crucial. Understanding that mistakes are a natural part of any relationship helps to break this cycle. Accepting your imperfections, learning from past experiences, and committing to personal growth are all steps toward forgiving yourself.

When it comes to forgiving your partner, it's important to acknowledge their humanity and recognize that they too can make mistakes. This process requires empathy, emotional maturity, and the ability to see the situation from their perspective. It may involve having difficult conversations, setting boundaries, and ensuring both partners are committed to rebuilding the relationship.

## The Power of Letting Go of Grudges

Holding onto a grudge not only harms your emotional well-being but also negatively impacts the quality of your relationship. When past hurts are continuously held onto, even after they have been addressed, it prevents true healing. A grudge keeps the wounds open, fueling resentment and obstructing the development of a deep connection.

On the other hand, letting go of grudges brings freedom. By consciously choosing to release negative emotions associated with past disputes, you create space for love, trust, and connection to grow. Letting go doesn't mean forgetting or ignoring the hurt but making the decision to stop letting those events define your relationship. This act of letting go is a gift to both your relationship and you, allowing you to fully engage with each other in a healthy, positive way.

## The Practice of Writing a Forgiveness Letter

One powerful technique for processing emotions and promoting healing is the act of writing a forgiveness letter. In this exercise, both partners write letters in which they either seek forgiveness for their actions that caused harm or express forgiveness for the past hurts they have experienced. This provides a safe space to express feelings that may be difficult to communicate verbally, allowing both individuals to reflect and gain clarity on what needs healing.

In these letters, you can express your desire to move forward, acknowledge the specific actions or behaviors that caused pain, and take responsibility for your mistakes. This includes expressing genuine remorse and outlining how you intend to make amends. Once exchanged, the letters can either be read aloud or reflected upon privately before discussing them. This practice fosters vulnerability, honesty, and a deeper emotional connection between partners.

## Healing Ritual for a New Beginning

A healing ritual serves as a symbolic act for couples to mark a new beginning after working through past hurts. By physically writing down lingering grievances, disappointments, or emotional scars and then performing a symbolic act to release them, such as burying, tearing, or burning the paper, both partners can express their commitment to starting anew.

This ritual signifies a willingness to let go of past pain and focus on rebuilding the relationship. It can be a powerful reminder that both individuals have chosen to prioritize healing and move forward with a fresh perspective. Engaging in this shared experience fosters closure and marks the beginning of a new chapter in the relationship.

## Summary

Forgiveness is a cornerstone of a lasting relationship, providing a path to healing and growth after conflict or betrayal. It's not about making excuses for bad behavior or disregarding the pain caused but about freeing both yourself and your partner from the weight of anger and resentment. By learning to forgive yourself and your partner, you can build a deeper emotional connection and trust. Letting go of grudges enables true healing and creates a stronger foundation for the future.

# CHAPTER 8:
# BALANCING INDEPENDENCE AND
# TOGETHERNESS

Understanding how to strike a healthy balance between preserving one's individuality and cultivating a shared identity is critical to the success of any love relationship throughout its longevity. It is equally essential for each partner to continue growing and developing as individuals, even though love and connection are the foundations upon which a partnership is built. When managed effectively, this balance between independence and togetherness enables both personal fulfillment and the growth of a successful partnership. In this chapter, we will discuss the importance of prioritizing personal development within a relationship, the risks associated with excessive independence or dependence, and how partners can create a healthy balance between "me time" and "we time."

## Key Ideas: Why Personal Growth is Important in a Relationship

The development of oneself within the context of a romantic partnership is essential to the well-being of both the individual and the relationship. When both partners continue to pursue their interests, passions, and personal ambitions, they contribute to a sense of fulfillment, confidence, and overall happiness. These positive emotions enhance the quality of the relationship. A partnership where both individuals are growing fosters a dynamic and enriched connection, capable of adapting to new circumstances and challenges.

Furthermore, when personal growth is prioritized, partners infuse fresh energy and experiences into the relationship, helping to prevent stagnation. Conversely, a lack of individual growth can lead to feelings of frustration or dissatisfaction. A partnership that encourages mutual support for individual goals builds a foundation of respect and admiration for each other's journeys, ultimately deepening the emotional connection.

## How Relationships Can Suffer from Excessive Independence or Dependence

While personal development is vital, excessive independence can damage a relationship. When partners prioritize their own lives to the detriment of the relationship, it can create emotional distance and lead to feelings of disconnection. If both partners are preoccupied with their individual pursuits, intimacy and closeness may diminish, causing the relationship to become secondary.

On the other hand, excessive dependence can also be detrimental. When one or both partners rely too heavily on the relationship for emotional support, validation, or fulfillment, it creates an unhealthy dynamic. This over-reliance can hinder personal growth and place undue strain on the relationship to meet all emotional needs. In severe cases, it may result in codependency, where the partnership ceases to be a source of mutual support and instead becomes a crutch.

The key is to find a balance between pursuing individual interests and nurturing the relationship. Both partners must feel free to pursue their unique passions while simultaneously investing in their connection. Ultimately, neither extreme—excessive independence nor excessive dependence—will lead to long-term satisfaction.

## Finding a Happy Medium Between "Me Time" and "We Time"

To create harmony between independence and togetherness, it is essential to strike the right balance between "me time" and "we time." "Me time" refers to periods when individuals focus on themselves—whether through hobbies, socializing with friends, or simply relaxing alone. "We time," on the other hand, encompasses moments couples dedicate to nurturing their relationship, such as engaging in shared activities, spending quality time together, or having meaningful conversations.

Open communication about each partner's needs is crucial in finding this balance. It's important to recognize that one partner may require more personal time than the other. For instance, one person might feel rejuvenated by solitude, while the other thrives on togetherness. Acknowledging and respecting these differences is essential while ensuring the relationship remains a priority.

Couples should also be mindful that the equilibrium between independence and togetherness may shift throughout their relationship, depending on life circumstances and relationship stages. Strategies that work in the early stages may need to evolve as the partnership develops. Flexibility and open communication are vital for navigating these changes successfully.

## Plan for Your Personal Space Exercises

The Personal Space Plan is designed to help couples articulate and communicate their needs for personal time and space clearly. Each partner takes time to reflect on the areas in which they require independent time, whether for hobbies, career, self-care, or simply to recharge. After noting these areas, couples meet to discuss their intentions and explore how they can accommodate each other's needs without feeling distant.

This exercise fosters a shared understanding of personal space, helping to prevent misunderstandings and feelings of neglect. It encourages couples to respect each other's individuality while ensuring both partners feel supported in their personal pursuits. By discussing these requirements openly, couples can establish boundaries that benefit both parties, leading to a healthier, more balanced relationship dynamic.

## The Challenge of Togetherness

For couples eager to prioritize "we time," the Togetherness Challenge is a fun and engaging way to enhance their connection. Each partner creates a list of activities they would like to share, such as weekend getaways, cooking classes, or watching favorite shows together. After compiling their lists, the couple commits to choosing one activity each week to enjoy together.

This activity reinforces the emotional bond between partners by ensuring that shared experiences remain a priority. It generates excitement and anticipation for quality time together, strengthening their connection. The Togetherness Challenge also fosters creativity and communication, encouraging couples to explore new ways to enjoy each other's company and create lasting memories.

## Summary

Striking a balance between independence and togetherness is essential for maintaining a healthy and fulfilling relationship. Personal growth allows each partner to thrive individually, introducing fresh energy and experiences into the partnership. However, excessive independence can lead to emotional detachment, while excessive dependence may foster an unhealthy dynamic. By finding a healthy balance between "me time" and "we time," both partners can develop as individuals while nurturing a strong connection as a couple.

# CHAPTER 9:
## OVERCOMING JEALOUSY AND INSECURITY

Jealousy and insecurity can be challenging emotions, yet they're a common experience for many couples. If left unaddressed, these feelings can gradually harm the relationship, weakening trust, intimacy, and connection. For instance, perhaps one partner feels uncomfortable with the other's friendships, or maybe self-doubt leads one to feel unworthy in the relationship. Recognizing and openly discussing these feelings can prevent misunderstandings and allow both partners to understand each other's needs more deeply.

In this chapter, we'll explore what drives feelings of jealousy and insecurity, offering tools to understand the root causes of these emotions. You'll find practical ways to communicate insecurities openly and constructively, as well as steps to strengthen self-confidence and build trust together. By working through these feelings, couples can address insecurities in a healthy way, fostering a stronger, more resilient relationship.

## Identifying the Fundamental Factors That Contribute to Jealousy

Jealousy is often rooted in deeper emotional scars, such as fear of abandonment, memories of past betrayals, or low self-esteem. When an individual perceives that their relationship or partner is at risk, whether the threat is real or imagined, jealousy can arise. For example, one might feel jealous when their partner spends time with a close friend, even without any reason to suspect inappropriate behavior. This form of jealousy is frequently linked to the individual's feelings of insecurity rather than their partner's actions.

The key to overcoming jealousy is to understand its underlying causes. Partners should reflect on whether their feelings of jealousy stem from external circumstances or internal emotions. By identifying these triggers, individuals can begin the healing process, ultimately leading to a stronger relationship. Often, jealousy is less about the partner and more about unresolved issues within oneself (Gottman, 2015).

## The Art of Communicating Insecurities Without Accusing Your Partner of Being Unfaithful

Conveying feelings of insecurity without resorting to accusations can be challenging but is essential for fostering a healthy relationship. When feeling insecure, individuals may project their feelings onto their partner, often resulting in accusations or blame. This approach rarely resolves the underlying issue and typically leads to defensiveness and conflict.

Instead, insecurities should be communicated in an open, non-confrontational manner. Using "I" statements can effectively express feelings without assigning blame. For instance, saying, "I feel insecure when you spend a lot of time with your friends because it makes me worry about our connection," is more constructive than, "You always spend time with your friends instead of me." This approach fosters an environment of vulnerability and encourages discussions about deeper feelings.

One crucial aspect of effective communication around insecurities is being explicit about what each partner needs for reassurance. Clearly voicing needs—be it for quality time, verbal affirmations, or transparency—enables both partners to understand how to support one another emotionally.

## A Guide to Developing Your Own Self-Confidence and Trust

Building self-confidence and trust, both individually and within the partnership, is vital in overcoming feelings of jealousy and insecurity. Self-confidence serves as the foundation upon which trust is built. When individuals are confident in themselves and what they contribute to the relationship, they are less likely to feel threatened by external factors. Pursuing personal interests, focusing on self-care, and setting goals that enhance self-image can all contribute to building self-confidence.

Trust, on the other hand, develops through consistent actions over time. Partners must demonstrate honesty, openness, and reliability. Trust is not something that can be established overnight; however, it can be rebuilt through collaborative efforts after a breach. Transparency involves being open about emotions and keeping promises. Simple acts like regular check-ins or expressing gratitude can reinforce trust.

Simultaneously, it is essential to have faith in oneself and the ability to navigate challenges within the relationship. Individuals are less likely to feel overwhelmed by jealousy or insecurity when they trust their judgment and emotional resilience.

## Jealousy Training and Reflection Exercises

The Jealousy Reflection exercise aims to assist partners in recognizing and addressing the factors that trigger feelings of insecurity and jealousy. Each partner takes time to reflect on instances where they experienced jealousy or insecurity, noting the specific circumstances that led to these feelings. Examples might include observing their partner with others, feeling neglected, or experiencing exclusion at social events.

After identifying these triggers, partners meet to discuss them openly and without judgment. The goal is to understand each other's emotional responses and develop strategies for managing these feelings in the future. For instance, if one partner feels insecure when the other spends time with friends, they might agree to schedule regular quality time together. This exercise promotes effective communication and helps couples empathize with each other's vulnerabilities.

## Summary

Jealousy and insecurity can undermine any relationship, eroding trust and intimacy if left unaddressed. However, couples can build deeper, more resilient connections by understanding the underlying causes of jealousy and learning to communicate insecurities without blame. Developing self-confidence and trust in oneself is a critical step in overcoming these emotional challenges.

By taking the time to reflect on their insecurities and communicate openly, couples can transform feelings of jealousy into opportunities for growth. In doing so, they create a partnership grounded in mutual trust, respect, and emotional security, enabling both partners to thrive individually and collectively.

# CHAPTER 10:

# FINANCIAL HARMONY: NAVIGATING

# MONEY IN RELATIONSHIPS

When it comes to relationships, one of the most prevalent sources of stress is financial issues. A variety of money-related concerns can put even the most solid partnerships under pressure. These disputes can arise over overspending, saving, or managing debt. For many couples, achieving financial harmony is challenging, particularly when each partner brings their own beliefs and practices regarding money into the relationship **(Markman, 2010)**. The purpose of this chapter is to investigate the influence that monetary matters have on romantic partnerships and explore ways partners can collaborate to achieve financial harmony. By encouraging open communication, aligning financial goals, and planning strategically together, couples can alleviate money-related tensions and strengthen their relationship.

## Frequently Encountered Financial Disagreements Between Couples: Key Concepts

In romantic partnerships, money can be a sensitive topic, especially when partners have differing financial interests or habits. Discrepancies in perspectives regarding spending and saving, disputes over debt management, and different budgeting methods are common financial issues. For instance, one partner may adopt a conservative approach, prioritizing savings for future goals, while the other may focus on enjoying the present and spending more freely. If these disagreements are not addressed early on, they can lead to frustration and conflict.

Another source of friction is the unequal distribution of financial resources. When one partner earns significantly more than the other, it may lead to feelings of guilt, anger, or power imbalances. To achieve financial harmony, couples must mutually understand and respect each partner's financial capabilities and responsibilities. It's important to recognize that financial harmony does not necessarily equate to equal contributions.

By identifying potential conflicts upfront, couples can approach issues in a manner that enhances their relationship rather than creating division. The first step in finding common ground is acknowledging that each person has a unique approach to managing finances.

## Approaches to Communicating About Money That Do Not Involve Conflict

To resolve financial issues before they escalate, it is essential to communicate about money openly and honestly. Conversations about finances can be unsettling, especially if one or both partners feel embarrassed or defensive about their financial habits. Couples should approach these discussions with empathy and a non-judgmental attitude.

A useful strategy is to establish regular financial check-ins, during which partners can openly discuss their current financial situation, goals, and concerns. Creating a secure and non-confrontational environment for these conversations allows both partners to express their thoughts and emotions without fear of judgment. Statements beginning with "I," such as "I feel stressed about our debt" or

"I want us to save more for our future," can help alleviate tension and facilitate meaningful dialogue.

Active listening during these discussions is equally important. Often, one partner may feel their concerns are unacknowledged, exacerbating financial issues. By demonstrating understanding and reassurance, couples can navigate their financial differences collaboratively. When partners perceive themselves as working together, they are more likely to approach financial challenges with a solution-focused mindset.

## Strategies for Planning Financial Matters as a Group

With open communication established, couples can proceed with financial planning as partners. Setting both short-term and long-term goals that reflect the values and priorities of both partners is crucial for financial planning. Whether the objective is to buy a home, pay off debt, save for retirement, or simply maintain a budget, creating a strategy to which both partners are committed is essential.

One effective approach is developing a combined budget that considers both individual and shared goals. This budget should account for each partner's financial obligations, including bills, savings contributions, and discretionary spending. Allocating finances for personal interests helps reduce feelings of resentment and ensures that neither partner feels deprived. Additionally, setting aside funds for shared experiences, such as vacations or date nights, can foster relationship growth.

Establishing a reserve for unexpected expenses is another critical aspect of financial planning. This safety net helps alleviate stress associated with unforeseen costs, such as medical bills or car repairs. Couples should also consider creating long-term financial plans for significant life events, such as home purchases, having children, or saving for retirement. By working together toward these goals, couples reinforce the idea that financial decision-making is a collaborative effort.

## Performing Financial Check-In Exercises

The Financial Check-In Exercise enables couples to assess their current financial situation and identify areas for improvement. Each partner should reflect on their financial habits, including spending, saving, and debt management. They can then come together to discuss their findings and how their financial choices align with their established goals.

During the check-in, partners should openly address any concerns or anxieties regarding their finances, including savings for the future and debt repayment progress. This exercise promotes transparency and accountability, allowing couples to navigate differences in financial perspectives. A mutual understanding of each other's financial routines empowers couples to make informed decisions about their relationship.

## Creating a Budget Together

The "Budgeting Together" activity is designed to help couples collaboratively create a budget that incorporates both individual and shared financial goals. Partners should begin by listing their monthly income, expenses, and financial objectives. They can then work together to develop a balanced budget that addresses essential needs, such as rent, utilities, groceries, and debt payments, while also allowing for savings and discretionary spending.

Throughout this process, partners should maintain a flexible mindset and be willing to make compromises. For example, if one partner prefers to save more aggressively while the other values spending on experiences, they can find common ground that balances both priorities. The goal is to create a budget that supports the financial health of the partnership while accommodating each partner's specific financial needs and preferences.

When it comes to relationships, money often serves as a significant source of conflict. However, achieving financial harmony is possible through open communication, common goal-setting, and strategic planning. Couples who understand frequent financial issues, such as differing spending habits or unequal contributions, can approach discussions about money with empathy and insight. Effective communication allows partners to share their financial concerns and collaborate on solutions.

Engaging in financial planning as a team—through budgeting and setting shared goals—ensures that both partners are aligned regarding their future. Activities like the Financial Check-In and Budgeting Together provide couples with valuable tools to evaluate their financial conditions and devise strategies for long-term stability and harmony. By working together and being transparent with one another, couples can reduce financial stress and lay a strong foundation for their future together.

## Summary

Finances play a crucial role in the health of romantic relationships, often becoming a source of stress when there are differing spending habits, unequal contributions, or conflicting approaches to debt.

Creating a budget together allows couples to clarify their individual and shared financial goals, reducing misunderstandings and building a collaborative financial plan. By working together on financial planning, couples can alleviate money-related stress, establish a foundation of financial stability, and strengthen their relationship for the future.

# CHAPTER 11:

# DEALING WITH EXTERNAL STRESSORS: FAMILY, WORK, AND FRIENDS

Stressors from the outside world can affect any relationship, whether they originate from family dynamics, workplace demands, or societal obligations. These external pressures can create tension within a relationship, especially if they are not addressed and managed effectively. It's easy for partners to project their frustrations onto each other or for the relationship itself to suffer when life outside the partnership becomes burdensome. In this chapter, we will explore how couples can protect their relationship against external stressors, establish healthy boundaries, and provide mutual support during challenging times.

# Establishing Boundaries with Family and Friends

Interactions with family and friends are significant sources of external stress in relationships. While these connections are important, they can inadvertently interfere with a couple's relationship if boundaries are not clearly defined. For instance, overly involved parents or demanding friends can create friction between partners when their influence feels overbearing or intrusive.

Establishing boundaries is crucial for maintaining the integrity of the relationship. Couples should communicate openly about areas where they need space from others and how they wish to handle outside pressures together. For example, one partner may feel uncomfortable with the time spent with in-laws, or there may be disagreements over how much friends should be involved in personal matters. By discussing these issues and agreeing on shared boundaries, couples can safeguard their relationship from external intrusions **(Tannen, 2007)**.

# Maintaining a Healthy Work-Life Balance to Avoid Burnout

Work-related stress is another significant external factor that can impact relationship quality. Long hours, demanding tasks, or work-related travel can leave little room for nurturing the partnership. Burnout can lead to frustration, low energy, and emotional distance, affecting both partners.

Couples need to discuss their professional obligations and find ways to prioritize their time together. This might involve setting limits on after-hours work, designating "work-free" times for connection, or mutually supporting improved work habits. Acknowledging the impact of work-related stress on the relationship is crucial for both partners to take proactive steps to ensure quality time together (Johnson, 2008).

## Methods for Providing Support During Stressful Times

During periods of external stress—such as family emergencies, work challenges, or societal pressures—partners must be available to support each other. Providing emotional support goes beyond mere presence; it requires understanding how each partner copes with stress and what they need during those times. Some may prefer solitude to process emotions, while others may seek verbal reassurance or physical comfort.

Patience and empathy are essential for effective support. It's important to approach behavioral changes with understanding rather than criticism **(Coontz, 2005)**. Regular check-ins can help partners remain attuned to each other's needs, ensuring that both feel supported and valued during challenging times.

## A Support Plan

The Support Plan exercise encourages couples to think about how they can support each other during stressful times. When one partner faces external pressures, the other identifies specific ways to provide emotional or practical support. For instance, if one partner's workload becomes overwhelming, they may need extra help with household tasks. Alternatively, they might appreciate time alone to decompress after a family disagreement.

**Type of Stressor:** Describe the external stressor affecting you.

Example: "Heavy workload for the upcoming project deadline."

**Requested Support:** Describe how you would like your partner to support you during this time.

Example: "Help with household tasks and understanding if I need extra quiet time."

**Exercise for Identifying Stressors and Support Needs**

To identify stressors and understand the support you each need, create a table on a separate sheet of paper with the following columns:

- **Type of Stressor**: List specific situations or challenges that cause stress for you (e.g., work deadlines, family issues, health concerns).

- **Requested Support**: Describe the type of support you'd appreciate from your partner when dealing with each stressor (e.g., listening without judgment, offering advice, helping with tasks).

After filling out your tables individually, come together to discuss your responses. Sharing these insights allows both partners to understand each other's needs better and find ways to support each other effectively.

This activity provides a clear roadmap for how to care for each other during stressful periods, reducing misunderstandings about the type of support needed.

By documenting their specific needs and discussing them, partners can enhance their ability to offer meaningful support. This activity provides a clear roadmap for how to care for each other during stressful periods, reducing misunderstandings about the type of support needed.

External stressors—such as family dynamics, job demands, and societal expectations—can significantly impact a relationship if not managed thoughtfully. Establishing boundaries with family and friends, achieving a healthy work-life balance, and providing mutual support during difficult times are essential strategies for maintaining a strong partnership in the face of external stress.

## Summary

External stressors—such as family dynamics, job demands, and societal expectations—can significantly impact a relationship if not managed thoughtfully. Establishing boundaries with family and friends, achieving a healthy work-life balance, and providing mutual support during difficult times are essential strategies for maintaining a strong partnership in the face of external stress.

# CHAPTER 12:

# SUSTAINING LONG-TERM

# RELATIONSHIP HAPPINESS

To maintain happiness in a long-term relationship, consistent effort, open communication, and a commitment to the partnership's growth are essential. Couples can easily become complacent, allowing routines to replace romance and excitement in their relationship. However, maintaining a healthy relationship over time is achievable through deliberate activities, ongoing development, and regular check-ins. In this chapter, we will discuss the crucial components necessary for keeping the flame alive, ensuring both partners grow together, and recognizing when it is time to refresh the connection.

# How to Maintain the Feeling of Romance in a Long-Term Relationship

As a relationship develops, the initial excitement often evolves into a deeper, more comfortable friendship. However, this does not mean that romance should be neglected. Couples can prioritize romance in their daily lives by incorporating small gestures, such as leaving sweet notes, planning surprise date nights, or discovering new hobbies to explore together. Engaging in shared activities that reignite their connection—like taking a dance class, cooking a new recipe, or going on weekend getaways—can be beneficial.

Moreover, maintaining a comfortable level of physical intimacy is crucial in long-term relationships. This encompasses not only sexual closeness but also affectionate gestures like hugs, kisses, and cuddling. Open communication about needs and desires can help partners feel more connected and valued. Prioritizing romantic moments fosters intimacy and strengthens the emotional bond between partners.

# The Importance of Continuous Growth and Learning Together

Continuous growth and development, both individually and as a couple, play a vital role in maintaining happiness in a long-term relationship. Encouraging and supporting each other in exploring new interests, hobbies, and personal ambitions contributes significantly to relationship success. Couples who learn and grow together are likely to maintain a strong bond, as they not only support each other's unique journeys but also share valuable experiences.

Participating in activities such as couples therapy, reading relationship books, or attending seminars can provide fresh ideas and strategies to deepen their connection. Moreover, cultivating a growth mindset enables partners to approach challenges with the understanding that personal and relational development is an ongoing journey. Embracing change and learning together can revitalize the relationship, leading to greater understanding and appreciation for one another throughout the process **(Hendrix, 2008)**.

## Recognizing Moments When the Relationship Requires a 'Time Out'

Recognizing when a relationship may need a "reset" is crucial for reigniting the connection. Every relationship experiences phases, and identifying when revitalization is necessary is key. Signs that a relationship may need rejuvenation include increased conflicts, feelings of distance, or a sense of monotony. It's essential to address these feelings rather than allowing them to fester.

A "reset" doesn't necessarily mean a complete overhaul; it involves being honest with oneself and communicating about what isn't working. This could involve discussing unresolved issues, revisiting agreed-upon goals, or simply taking time to reconnect without distractions. A "relationship retreat" can provide partners with dedicated time to focus entirely on each other and the relationship, away from the stresses of daily life. Couples may consider introducing this type of time.

## The Reset Button

The *Relationship Vision Board* activity allows couples to collaboratively reimagine and refresh their relationship by visualizing their ideal future together. Unlike traditional goal-setting, this activity encourages creativity, imagination, and shared dreams, helping partners reconnect on an aspirational level.

### Step 1: Set Up a Creative Space

- **Gather Supplies**: Collect magazines, photos, markers, glue, and a large piece of paper or poster board. If you prefer digital tools, use an app to create a virtual board.

- **Choose a Relaxed Setting**: Find a comfortable, distraction-free space where you both feel at ease to be creative.

## Step 2: Brainstorm Together

- **Reflect on Your Ideal Relationship**: Take turns sharing what an "ideal future" together looks like. Think beyond daily routines—explore dreams, personal growth, new experiences, and long-term goals.

- **Prompt Questions**:

  - "What activities would we love to do together more often?"

  - "What values and habits would strengthen our connection?"

  - "What new experiences do we want to create together?"

  - "How would our relationship feel if it was in the best place it could be?"

**Step 3: Create Your Vision Board**

- **Select Images and Words**: Choose images, quotes, or words that resonate with your shared vision. This could include representations of places you want to visit, activities to try, or symbols that reflect your relationship's values.

- **Arrange and Design**: Arrange the images and words on the board in a way that visually represents your ideal relationship. This part is open-ended—there's no right or wrong way to create your board!

**Step 4: Discuss and Commit to Key Elements**

- **Highlight Key Aspects**: Once your board is complete, identify a few themes or items that stand out as most meaningful. Discuss how you can start integrating these elements into your relationship in small ways.

  - **Examples**:

    - If "adventure" is a theme, plan a monthly date where you try something new together.

- If "quality time" is a priority, commit to technology-free time together each evening.

- If "growth" is a focus, consider joining a class or workshop you're both interested in.

**Step 5: Display Your Vision Board**

- **Place It Somewhere Visible**: Keep your vision board somewhere you'll both see it regularly, as a reminder of your shared aspirations.

- **Use It as a Reference**: Periodically check in with the board to see how you're doing on your shared goals and if there's anything new you'd like to add.

This vision board exercise allows couples to reconnect and set intentions in a fun, visual way. By building a shared vision, couples can refresh their connection and align on a future that feels exciting and fulfilling for both partners.

## Summary

Happiness in a long-term relationship is not a passive state; it requires continuous effort, communication, and mutual commitment. By actively maintaining romance, embracing the idea of continuous growth together, and recognizing when a reset is necessary, couples can cultivate a vibrant and fulfilling relationship. The activities described in this chapter, such as the Relationship Maintenance Plan and the Reset Button, provide couples with valuable tools to sustain their happiness. Ultimately, enduring joy is attainable when both partners invest in their connection and prioritize the process of growing and loving one another.

# CONCLUSION

As we conclude our investigation into the complex world of relationships, it is of the utmost importance to acknowledge the fact that love is not only a destination but rather an ongoing journey. We have investigated the many different aspects of relationships throughout the pages of this book, including communication, trust, intimacy, and more. Each chapter has revealed important insights and practical techniques that can assist couples in navigating their pathways. Love, on the other hand, is a dynamic and ever-evolving adventure that requires both parties to maintain a constant commitment to growth and understanding throughout the relationship.

Challenges and roadblocks are something that will be encountered in every relationship. The strength of your connection may be put to the test during these moments, but they may also act as a catalyst for growth and a stronger connection between you. Always keep in mind that patience is the most important quality to possess since it enables you to handle disagreements with poise and creates an atmosphere in which both partners feel heard and respected. It is through open communication, honesty, and mutual respect that relationships can flourish. The cultivation of these aspects not only strengthens the emotional connection between the two of you but also provides the groundwork for a durable partnership that is able to sustain itself over time.

One other essential element that contributes to the success of a relationship is trying. When you make a conscious decision to put time and energy into your relationship, you may revive the passion and excitement that brought you together in the first place. It is easy to fall into routines and become complacent, but active choices can help you do so. It is possible to keep the flame of love alive with activities such as regular check-ins, late evenings, and shared goals. To reinforce the idea that love is founded on teamwork and collaboration, it is important to celebrate the tiny wins and praise the efforts that each partner contributes.

The third component that is necessary for a healthy partnership is dedication. A commitment that is unshakeable to both your spouse and the relationship is required for it to be successful. This commitment entails being there for one another at challenging times, providing support and encouragement to one another through the process of growing both as individuals and as a partnership. It is about having the realization that love is not always simple but that the benefits of having a profound and significant relationship far transcend the difficulties that are encountered along the path.

Ultimately, love is a journey that is full of unexpected turns and twists, and it requires patience, work, and attention from both parties in the relationship. As you make your way through this trip, it is important to keep in mind that you should always put your relationship first, that you should learn from the challenges you face, and that you should treasure the moments of delight. You can construct a long-lasting relationship that not only endures the test of time but also flourishes with each passing day if you are willing to embrace the process and make a commitment to the journey together. Love, in all of its manifestations, is an investment that is well worth making, and as you move forward, may you never stop developing, learning, and flourishing together.

# Thank You

Thank you so much for taking the time to read this workbook. I truly hope the insights, exercises, and reflections within these pages help you build a deeper, more fulfilling relationship. Remember that every relationship is unique, and the key to long-lasting love is nurturing it with care, understanding, and consistent effort. May you find success, happiness, and growth on your journey together.

If you found value in this book, I would greatly appreciate it if you could take a moment to leave a review on Amazon. Your feedback not only helps other readers but also inspires me to continue sharing and writing.

Wishing you all the best in your relationship and beyond!

# Exclusive Online Test

Thank you for exploring this workbook together. To enhance your journey, we've included exclusive tests designed to help you and your partner deepen your understanding of each other. Simply scan the QR code below to access these valuable exercises and continue strengthening your bond, or follow the link:

www.relationshipquizforcouples.com

# References

1. Chapman, G. (2015). The 5 love languages: The secret to love that last. Northfield Publishing.

2. Gottman, J., & Silver, N. (2015). The seven principles for making marriage work: A practical guide from the country's foremost relationship expert. Harmony Books.

3. Lerner, H. (2004). The dance of connection: How to talk to someone when you're mad, hurt, scared, frustrated, insulted, betrayed, or desperate. HarperCollins.

4. Perel, E. (2017). The state of affairs: Rethinking infidelity. HarperCollins.

5. Markman, H. J., Stanley, S. M., & Blumberg, S. L. (2010). Fighting for your marriage: Positive steps for preventing divorce and preserving a lasting love. Jossey-Bass.

6. Sbarra, D. A., & Hazan, C. (2008). Relationship dissolution, social support, and health. In J. P. Forgas & J. Fitness (Eds.), Social relationships: Cognitive, affective, and motivational processes (pp. 335-356). Psychology Press.

7. Tannen, D. (2007). You just don't understand: Women and men in conversation. Harper Paperbacks.

8. Wile, D. B. (2002). After the honeymoon: How conflict can improve your relationship. Columbia University Press.

9. Tatkin, S. (2011). Wired for love: How understanding your partner's brain and attachment style can help you defuse conflict and build a secure relationship. New Harbinger Publications.

10.    Fisher, H. (2004). Why we love: The nature and chemistry of romantic love. Henry Holt and Co.

11. Covey, S. R. (1998). The 7 habits of highly effective families: Building a beautiful family culture in a turbulent world. St. Martin's Press.

12. Coontz, S. (2005). Marriage, a history: How love conquered marriage. Viking Penguin.

13. Hendrix, H. (2008). Getting the love you want: A guide for couples. Henry Holt and Co.

14. Johnson, S. M. (2008). Hold me tight: Seven conversations for a lifetime of love. Little, Brown and Company.

Made in the USA
Las Vegas, NV
11 February 2025

17885817R00057